DATE DUE

DEMCO 38-297

WORLD IN VIEW
EGYPT

Ian A. Morrison

STECK-VAUGHN
L I B R A R Y

Austin, Texas

Library of Congress Cataloging-in-Publication Data

Morrison, Ian A.
    Egypt / Ian A. Morrison.
        p.   cm.—(World in view)
    Includes index.
    Summary: A survey of Egypt's history, geography, industries, economy, people, and problems.
    ISBN 0-8114-2445-6
    1. Egypt—Juvenile literature. [1. Egypt.]
  I. Title. II. Series.
  DT49.M67   1991
  962—dc20   91-7791
                                        CIP AC

Cover: *Camel and rider at the pyramids, Giza:* James Davis Travel Photography
Title page: *Snake charmers in Cairo market*

Designed by Julian Holland Publishing Ltd.
Picture research by Jennifer Johnson

Typeset by Multifacit Graphics, Keyport, NJ
Printed and bound in the United States
by Lake Book, Melrose Park, IL
1 2 3 4 5 6 7 8 9 0 LB 95 94 93 92 91

Photographic Credits
All photos have been supplied by the author

Contents

1. Land of Contrasts   5
2. The Empty Red Land   12
3. The Nile   19
4. Agriculture and the Black Land   28
5. The World of the Pharaohs   34
6. Egyptians and Outsiders   43
7. Egypt's Recent History   52
8. Development and Industry   61
9. Cities, Towns, and Transportation   69
10. Problems and Solutions   76
11. Egyptian Life Today   83
12. Egypt's Gifts to the World   91
    Index   95

EGYPT

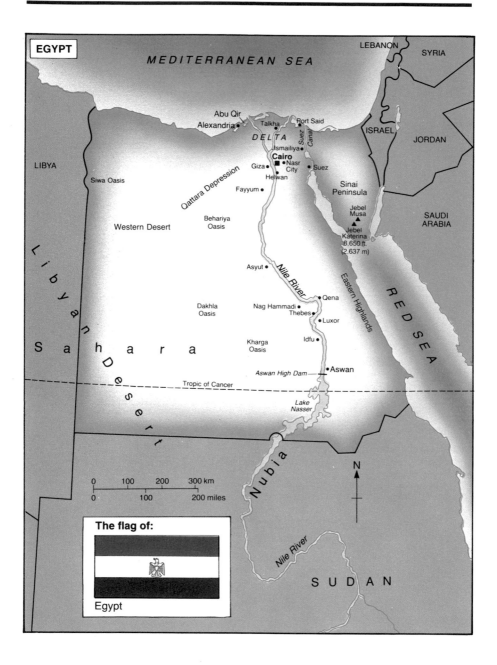

EGYPT

LEBANON
SYRIA

MEDITERRANEAN SEA

Abu Qir
Alexandria •
Talkha • • Port Said
DELTA
• Ismailiya
Cairo ■
Giza • • Nasr City
Hellwan •
• Suez

ISRAEL
JORDAN

LIBYA

Siwa Oasis

Qattara Depression

Fayyum •

Western Desert

Behariya Oasis

Sinai Peninsula

Jebel Musa
▲
▲ Jebel Katerina
8,650 ft.
(2,637 m)

SAUDI ARABIA

Asyut •

Nile River

• Qena

Dakhla Oasis

Nag Hammadi •
Thebes •
• Luxor

Eastern Highlands

RED SEA

Kharga Oasis

Idfu •

• Aswan

Aswan High Dam —

Tropic of Cancer

Lake Nasser

L i b y a n

S   a   h   a   r   a

D e s e r t

Nubia

N

| 0 | 100 | 200 | 300 km |
| 0 | | 100 | 200 miles |

Nile River

S U D A N

The flag of:

Egypt

4

1   Land of Contrasts

Egypt is a land of contrasts, surprises, and contradictions. When people hear the name, they tend to think of an ancient land with pyramids built for the pharaohs. It is true that Egypt was one of the first places in the world where a civilization developed. However, in other ways it is a very young country. Nearly half its people are less than 15 years of age, and while some lifestyles still seen there go back thousands of years, it is a country of very rapid change in our present oil age. Egypt does not have much oil of its own, yet life there is influenced by the oil wealth of other countries, and many Egyptians go abroad to jobs created by oil money elsewhere.

The Middle East
Egypt lies in what is called the Middle East. This term is commonly used to describe the countries from Iran in the northeast to Egypt in the west. The willingness of Egyptians to work elsewhere in the Middle East is partly because they share the

---

The Name of Egypt
The official name of Egypt is now the Arabic Republic of Egypt, or *Jumhuriyat Misr al-Arabiya.*

The English word "Egypt" comes from the ancient Egyptian *Het-ka-ptah, Ka* being the word for soul and *ptah* being one of their gods. When the Greeks ruled Egypt they changed *Het-ka-ptah* to *Ai-gy-ptious*, from which we get "Egypt."

Fact Box

Area: 386,900 sq. miles (1,001,449 sq. km.)

Population: 54,780,000 (1989 est.)

Capital city: Cairo

Language: the official language is Arabic, although French and English are widely used, especially for business.

Currency: the gold Egyptian pound, divided into 100 *piastras* made up of 1,000 *milliémes*

Egypt's flag: this dates from the time of President Nasser (1954–1970). At that time Egypt wished to emphasize that it was one of the Arab nations. It changed its flag to one with three bands in red, white, and black that is used by a number of Arab countries. Egypt's flag is distinguished by an eagle in the middle of the white band.

language of Arabic with many other countries there. With well over 50 million people, Egypt has by far the largest Arabic-speaking population. The next four most populated Arabic states are Iraq, Saudi Arabia, Syria, and the Yemen Arab Republic, but even added together their populations come to less than that of Egypt.

Despite this, Egypt is not located in the traditional homeland of the Arabs, the Arabian Peninsula between the Red Sea and the Gulf. Instead, Egypt is in the northeast corner of Africa, with the Red Sea to the east and the Mediterranean Sea to the north. There, along the Nile River, the Egyptians have been able to develop in their own particular way, set apart from their neighbors by the deserts on either side.

Ancient and modern, side by side: the temple of Sobek the Crocodile God at Kom Ombo is overshadowed by the present-day smoke of industry, while the Black Land by the Nile continues to be farmed as it has been since long before the temple was built.

However, although this isolation has been important, so has the fact that since ancient times the Nile has provided a route linking the Mediterranean and Middle East with the heart of Africa. The international importance of Egypt was increased by the building of the Suez Canal, which links the Mediterranean and Red seas, and thus beyond them the lands around the Atlantic and Indian oceans.

Red and Black lands

Further contradictions and contrasts are to be found within Egypt itself. It is at once an empty and a crowded country. There are vast stretches of desert wastes where nobody lives. These have changed very little since the early rulers of Egypt,

In Upper Egypt, there is often very little space between the edge of the Nile and the start of the desert. The river has cut into the landscape, so that the valley bottom is often lined by steep slopes and cliffs. This topography means that in many places it is not practicable to enlarge the area that is farmed, despite Egypt's increasingly serious shortage of food.

the pharaohs, referred to them as the Red Land of Egypt: red because of the color of the barren desert sands. This was in contrast to what the pharaohs called the Black Land, the inhabitable strip watered by the Nile and enriched by the dark organic muds deposited by the river. Many of the people of Egypt (perhaps four out of ten) still work the land, with the *fellahin* (the Arabic word for peasant farmers) living in population densities often as high as in the rice-paddy lands of Asia. However, it is not just peasant farmers that the Nile has supported on its Black Land. Alexandria has been a sophisticated city since ancient times. Cairo, the capital of Egypt, is now one of the largest cities in the world. People are crowded into parts of Cairo more densely than in New York City's skyscrapers.

Cairo is now one of the world's biggest and busiest cities. Its buses move over three million commuters each day, but the drivers still have to watch out for camels in the streets.

Thus, whether they are farming villagers or city dwellers, almost everybody lives on the floodplain of the Nile River. This means that nine out of ten Egyptians live crowded into only three percent of the country's area. The contrast between the emptiness of the Red Land and the concentration of people on the Black Land that was so familiar a part of life to the ancient Egyptians is thus even more marked today.

Egyptian Animals

There used to be many more kinds of wild animals in Egypt than there are today. It is difficult to be sure how much this is due to changes in the climate, and how much to people hunting the animals. Certainly, about 5,000 years ago, the elephant, rhinoceros, giraffe, and wild camel disappeared from many parts of the country. Lions and leopards were already becoming rare in Egypt by then. However, they were still hunted in the times of the pharaohs, along with ostriches, wild asses, oryx, ibex, and several kinds of desert gazelle and antelope. The pharaohs still hunted the hippopotamus for sport in the swamps of the Nile River, though even then it had become sufficiently rare.

Horus, the Hawk God, was one of the most important of all the ancient gods.

The Nile crocodile was held in awe in ancient times as well as in modern times. Sobek was a god with a crocodile head. There is a large temple in his honor at Kom Ombo, and there was even an ancient town called Krokodilopolis. The ancient Egyptians used to mummify their holy crocodiles, like these at Kom Ombo.

For the Nile crocodiles, it was humans who were sometimes the food animal. In spite of this, the ancient Egyptians regarded them as holy beasts, preserved their bodies as mummies, had a god with a crocodile head, and even named the town of Krokodilopolis after them!

The Nile is still a paradise for birds, despite centuries of trapping and hunting. However, most of the larger wild animals that once lived along the river are now gone because of the pressure of such a dense population. Some of the antelopes and gazelles have survived until the present century due to their ability to cope with drought and live far out in the almost waterless deserts.

2   The Empty Red Land

The Nile, with its narrow strip of well-watered Black Land, flows from south to north through Egypt. It runs nearer to the east side of the country, so the western desert is Egypt's greatest area of Red Land. However, in the east, both the Sinai Peninsula to the north and the Eastern Highlands farther south are very dry, too. Only one in every ten Egyptians lives away from the Nile, and most of the people who do live out in the Red Land stay grouped near oases, where they can get water in the desert. This leaves much of the Red Land entirely empty of people.

A hot and dry climate

This emptiness and barrenness away from the Nile is hardly surprising, because Egypt lies in one of the hottest and driest parts of the world. To the west are the Libyan and Sahara deserts, while to the east are the great deserts of Saudi Arabia. The only area in Egypt with reasonably reliable rainfall is a narrow strip scarcely 50 miles (80 kilometers) wide along the coast in the north where moisture blows off the Mediterranean Sea. Even in the coastal strip, only four to eight inches (100 to 200 millimeters) of rain fall in most years, and the heat of the sun can soon evaporate that amount. At Alexandria, Egypt's main coastal city, daily temperatures often rise to 86°F (30°C), despite the cooling effect of the sea.

Throughout the rest of the country, the true Red Land, the rainfall is almost always less than two inches (50 millimeters) per year, and in many

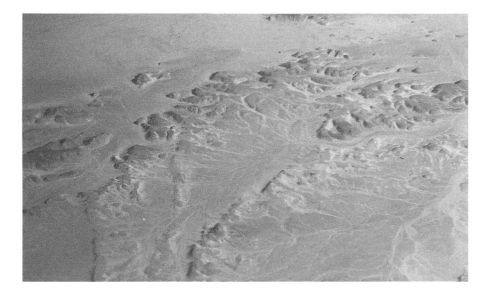

Part of the Western Desert, as empty as Mars, the red planet.

areas no rain at all may fall for years on end. At Cairo, which is only about 100 miles (170 kilometers) south of the coast, the average rainfall is less than one inch (22 millimeters) a year, and heavy showers may come only once in two or three years. Southern Egypt gets even less rain than the northern part of the country; Aswan has an official average rainfall of 0.04 of an inch (1 millimeter!), which means that for all practical purposes there is no useful rainfall at all. In places like Aswan, far from the cooling influence of the sea, it is not unusual to have summer temperatures of 108°F (42°C) or more.

These hot and dry conditions can be made even worse anywhere in Egypt when a hot wind, known as the Khamaseen, blows dust storms out of the Sahara desert. This wind most often occurs in April and May or August and September.

13

The Khamaseen

The "Santa Annas" of California and the "Brickfielders" of Australia are hot and nasty winds, but they are on a smaller scale than the Egyptian Khamaseen.

When the Khamaseen wind blows out of the desert, temperatures may rise by over 40°F (20°C) in a few hours. Crops wither, people suffer nervous tension, and the death rate rises, particularly among babies. Static electricity, which results from the storm, can interrupt communications, and the dust carried by the winds makes it difficult to see. The ancient Greek historian Herodotus tells of a Persian army that set out into the desert to attack the Egyptian oasis of Siwa but lost its way in a Khamaseen and was never heard of again. The driving sand and dust can bury roads and may also rise thousands of feet into the atmosphere, putting aircraft at risk. Sometimes this dust is carried great distances. In recent years reddish-colored Saharan dust has fallen on southern England.

It is not just dust and sand that may be whirled into the air. Where the storm sweeps across a marshy oasis or lake, there have been cases of small creatures being swept up, so that it has literally rained frogs and fishes (though not cats and dogs!).

The Western Desert

The Western Desert has as its foundation part of one of the massive plates of tough rock, hundreds of millions of years old, that make up much of the continent of Africa. Lying flat on top are shallow layers of more recent rocks, holding some oil and natural gas. These level rocks create vast expanses of desert plain without any big mountains. About half the Western Desert lies below 660 feet (200 meters), and few parts are more than 1,000 feet (300 meters) above sea level. There are some inland basins with floors well below the level of the sea. In a rainier climate, these would fill up as great lakes.

The largest of these basins is the Qattara Depression, which covers many thousands of square miles, southwest of Alexandria. Parts of its floor are actually around 400 feet (120 meters) below sea level. Water in the rock seeps to the surface there, but the sun is so hot that instead of forming a lake, most of the water evaporates, leaving a salt marsh. At Fayyum, nearer Cairo, there is enough water for a lake, and well over a million people farm there. There are other basins out in the desert where water can be pumped up to form oases so that crops can be grown. The main oases are Dakhla, Kharga, Behariya, and Siwa, but only a few thousand people live at each of these.

Outside the basins, the vast expanse of the desert is virtually empty of people, as it has been since ancient times. Sometimes, in gravelly areas, the undisturbed tracks of those who passed through tens or even hundreds of years before can still be seen. Some people think they have identified wheel marks left by Napoleon's cannons during the French invasion of Egypt in 1798, and tank tracks from the battles of World War II are certainly there. Although much of the Western Desert is stony, sand becomes more plentiful toward the southwest. This terrain makes it hard to move between Egypt and Libya.

The Sinai Peninsula

"Peninsula" means "almost an island," and the Sinai Peninsula fits this description. It is a triangular region of desert next to Israel, separated from the rest of Egypt by the Red Sea and the Suez Canal. The Sinai acts as a bridge between northeast Africa and southwest Asia plus the Arabian Peninsula. This land-bridge has been a battlefield since ancient times, with the discovery of oil further raising tensions. As recently as 1967, Sinai was seized by Israel and was not returned fully to Egypt until 1982. The peninsula rises into mountains that include Jebel Musa or Mount Sinai, mentioned in the Bible. Another mountain in the area is Jebel Katherina, Egypt's highest point at 8,650 feet (2,637 meters).

The Eastern Highlands

The Eastern Highlands, lying between the Nile Valley and the Red Sea, reach a height of 7,170 feet (2,185 meters). Overall, however, they are much lower, averaging 1,600 feet (500 meters). Like the Sinai, they are cut up by complicated patterns of steep-sided waterless valleys (called wadis), and few routes cross the area. The rugged scenery of the Eastern Highlands is partly due to the geological faults that crisscross the area. For millions of years, these have been on the move, and there are still earthquakes in the region.

There is little water in the ground in the Eastern Highlands and almost no useful rainfall, so there is no farming. The few inhabitants work in mining camps or in new tourist resorts being developed along the coast. In the past, few towns grew up along the Red Sea coast of Egypt for two

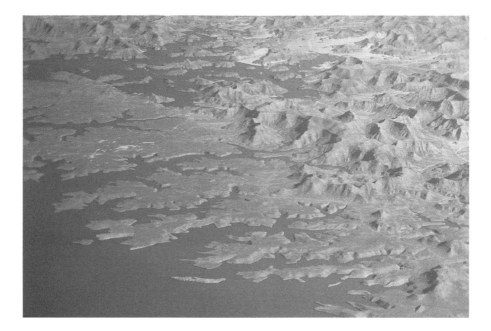

When Lake Nasser was created, it overflowed the cliffs along the Nile, flooding onto the surrounding Red Land. However, the water did not create new farmlands there. It merely wet the barren desert sand, and the evaporation has left white salt crusts.

reasons. One was the shortage of drinking water. The other reason was that its fringe of coral reefs made it a difficult coast for ships to navigate. It is only recently, with the worldwide popularity of scuba diving, that these spectacular reefs have offered the Egyptians the possibility of bringing in much-needed foreign money by creating new resorts catering to diving vacations.

On and offshore there is oil, and in the Eastern Highlands there are also minerals, including phosphates, from which fertilizers are made. Metals such as iron and gold are also found. Although iron is more important now, gold is still extracted from some of the same places, such as the Wadi Hammamat, where it was mined to ornament the mummies of the pharaohs.

17

The wind is more important in shaping the landscape of the Red Land than in wetter lands. These dark rock outcrops have been scoured by wind blown sand.

Agatharchides, an ancient Greek writer, tells of the horrible working conditions of the convicts in the mines. Some of the tunnels were so narrow that only children or persons starved nearly to skeletons could have crept through.

Desert plants

Much of the Red Land has very little or no plant life. The plants that can survive there are ones like the camel-thorn. Large, soft leaves would soon shrivel up in the desert, so the plants that are found have tough, narrow spikes that do not catch the sun with a leathery or waxy skin that prevents their moisture from evaporating. Many desert plants can appear to be dead for years on end, but when a shower of rain eventually does come, they flower quickly and set seeds. These seeds are in turn able to survive years of drought until the next shower.

3   The Nile

The Nile is often over a half-mile wide, wider in many places than the land it waters before the desert starts. The river remains the main "artery" of Egypt's body. Along the horizon stride pylons, carrying electricity generated by the river turbines of the Aswan High Dam to Cairo and the modern industries far to the north.

The Nile River is vital to Egypt's agriculture. In ancient times, Herodotus called Egypt "the gift of the Nile," and this is just as true now as in the past. It is not just a matter of agriculture. Without the Nile, there would be no water to support the modern cities of Egypt and their industries. Certainly Cairo, surrounded as it is by desert, could not have developed into what is now one of the largest cities in the world if it did not stand on one of the world's major rivers.

The smaller rivers, or tributaries, that come together to make up the Nile start far away from Egypt, deep in Africa. In order of increasing length, the main tributaries are the Atbara, the

19

Blue Nile, and the White Nile. The most remote part of the White Nile is the Luvironza River, which rises south of the equator in the central African state of Burundi. From there to the Mediterranean, the Nile is 4,160 miles (6,695 kilometers) long—the longest river in the world. The Nile gathers water from a drainage basin covering 750,000 square miles (nearly 2 million square kilometers). Only a very small part of the huge amount of water collected in the drainage basin is available to the Egyptians, however, because it is evaporated by the heat of the sun and seeps away into the ground. This happens both as the river passes through Africa on its way to Egypt and in Egypt itself. In summertime, even between Aswan and Cairo, nearly half the river's water may be lost. As much as 27 percent of the water is evaporated by the sun and at least 15 percent seeps away into the rocks.

The farming year in the past
In most parts of the world, the pattern of the farming year is set by each area's weather. The times of planting and harvest depend on local temperatures, or when the rainy season is at that particular place. In Egypt there is no problem with frost and, since there is virtually no useful rainfall, the pattern of farming life each year used to be set not by local conditions but by when the Nile flood arrived. The timing of the river's floods was controlled by events far away in the tributaries of the Nile in Africa. The level of the Nile in Egypt was lowest during May and early June. Then the water from the late spring and early summer rainy season to the south arrived.

The Nilometer at Aswan, a measuring device, was used when the river flooded in through the door each year. Its height could be measured on a scale set in the wall to the right of the doorway. From the height the flood reached, the pharaohs could forecast how much land would get enough water to grow crops, and could set their taxes accordingly. The rounded rock is hard granite that caused cataracts (rapids) in the river and from which obelisks were carved.

The first contribution to arrive was from the White Nile, but soon much more water was added by the Blue Nile and the Atbara. The flood increased rapidly through July and August, reaching its highest level in mid-September. At Aswan, the flooded river often rose 33 feet (10 meters) above its dry-season level. Then the water level would fall quickly throughout October and November and remain low between December and mid-June. The main planting of crops, such as wheat and barley, beans and chickpeas, took place as soon as the floods receded. The first crops were ready for harvest in January or February, when it was still frosty winter in Europe across the Mediterranean.

The size of the flood that came down the Nile in

21

any particular year was critical for the Egyptians. If the rains in Africa failed so that the Nile floods were low, not enough of the Black Land would be watered to feed the population. Then people starved. The Old Testament describes such lean years in Biblical times, even though there were many fewer mouths to feed then.

The Aswan High Dam

The building of the Aswan High Dam to make Lake Nasser in the south of Egypt has been far the largest and most important event to affect the Nile River since ancient times. Before this enormous reservoir existed, the Egyptians were entirely dependent on whatever rains fell each year farther south in Africa, as explained above. The reservoir can now store water from year to year, so that extra water from earlier years can be used when the African rains fail. There are other advantages, too. Within each year the water can be released more evenly, instead of coming down in a single flood. This allows more than one crop to be taken every year from much of the Black Land. Huge turbines, which can make electricity as water flows over them, are set into the dam. The hydroelectricity produced is another valuable benefit. The High Dam was started in 1958 with engineers and money from the Soviet Union. The reservoir began to store water in 1964, and the project was completed in 1971.

Lake Nasser is some 310 miles (500 kilometers) long and stretches back over the border into the Sudan. The reservoir now covers nearly 2,000 square miles (5,000 square kilometers), flooding a large part of the region known as Nubia.

Problems Created by Damming the Nile

The building of the Aswan High Dam and the creation of Lake Nasser has brought many advantages, but has also brought serious problems to Egypt. Some were expected and accepted as a price worth paying for the advantages. Others have come as surprises. Some of the problems are listed below.

● The fertile strip of Black Land in Nubia, above the dam, was flooded and lost beneath Lake Nasser. Ancient monuments were drowned beneath the water or moved at great expense, as at Abu Simbel. The Nubian people who have lived in this area since ancient times had to leave. Some were resettled at Kom Ombo, lower down the Nile, but many went to find work in Cairo.

● The valuable mud, which in the past created and fertilized the Black Land, is now being caught by the dam and is gradually choking the reservoir. The mud is also not available for farming. Egyptian farmers must now spend a great deal of money on fertilizers for the lands downstream of the dam.

● The mud that came down to the delta each year used to build it out into the sea. Now that the supply of mud has stopped, there are problems with erosion of the delta. The sardine fishing off the delta has also been spoiled, and attempts to build up fish-breeding in Lake Nasser have met with problems.

● Now that the great annual flood is no longer allowed to sweep down the length of the Nile, water snails are working their way upstream spreading bilharzia. This is a particularly nasty parasite that affects people working in irrigated lands.

Like many other ancient sites, the temples at Abu Simbel would have been submerged when Lake Nasser was created. However, in a UNESCO rescue operation completed in 1968, they were sawed into blocks and reassembled above the shoreline of the lake.

A fertile valley

Once it passes north of Aswan and heads for Cairo, the Nile flows quietly through a valley set between cliffs. These are seldom much more than six miles (ten kilometers) apart. The cliffs mark the border between the fertile Black Land of the river valley and the Red Land of the deserts to either side. The valley gets some shelter from the scorching winds of the desert above, but the cliffs limit the size of the cultivated area. Sometimes the farmable land is only several hundred feet wide. The river, which itself is often over a half-mile wide, tends to flow closer to the eastern valley wall. Thus most of the cultivated land lies west of the Nile, although the river loops from side to side.

With modern diesel pumps, water can be pumped to lands high above the river level, although at a cost. However, irrigation is pointless where there is no good soil, but only the barren sand and grit of the Red Land. The rich Black Land goes no higher than the level the river used to reach in time of flood, for it is made up of alluvium. This is the word for mud laid down by a river.

In the case of the Nile, the alluvium was particularly rich in chemicals, which made the land fertile and good for growing crops. The White Nile flows through great mats of plants called *sudd*, in the Sudan, which put green organic matter into the river water. The Atbara and Blue Nile added valuable fresh minerals worn away from rocks of volcanic areas, for

Today big diesel pumps are used to lift irrigation water out of the Nile onto the Black Land. They are often mounted on rafts so that they can be moved easily from place to place. The metal pillars have insets at several heights, so that the pump can still be connected whether the level of the Nile is high or low.

Although great efforts have been made to install piped supplies of safe drinking water throughout Egypt, many villagers still draw water from the Nile for household purposes as well as to irrigate their fields.

example in Ethiopia. This made the Nile floods important not only for the water itself but also for the fertilizing mud laid down each year. The mud had other advantages, too. It is soft when it first comes from the river, but it soon hardens in the sun and can be used to make banks for irrigation canals or mud-brick houses.

The river delta

Below Cairo the Nile escapes from the cliffs and spreads out into the Mediterranean Sea in a great delta. The word is taken from the Greek letter *delta*, which is written as a triangle. This is the shape on the map that often results where a river fans out when it meets the sea. The Nile is a big river, and its delta is also a large one—155 miles from west to east and 100 miles from south to north (250 by 160 kilometers).

A large proportion of the food grown in Egypt comes from the delta lands. The Egyptian government is worried about the possible consequences of the so-called "greenhouse effect," or the heating of the Earth's atmosphere due to pollution. Many scientists believe this heating will melt parts of the Arctic and Antarctic ice sheets, and the extra water the melting ice produces will cause a rise in world ocean levels. It has been estimated that Egypt might lose more than 20 percent of its farmland if a rising sea level submerged the delta. This loss of land would obviously be very serious for a poor country that already has problems in feeding its rapidly growing population.

4 Agriculture and the Black Land

Although more meat is eaten in Egypt now than in the past, animals are still largely used for working the land, sometimes using types of wooden plows that have changed little for thousands of years. Because many of the land holdings are very small and many of the people are poor, there is relatively little mechanized farming.

Perhaps four out of ten people in Egypt still work the land, and many others earn their living from industries based on agricultural products. In the farming areas of Egypt, population densities are often as high as in the rice-paddy lands of southeastern Asia.

In some ways, the lifestyles of many of the villagers who work the land have altered remarkably little since the times of the pharaohs. In other respects, however, life on the Black Land is now changing very rapidly. Since the creation of the Aswan High Dam and Lake Nasser, the

flow of water in the Nile River through Egypt can be controlled. This ability has altered life in Egypt in complicated and sometimes unexpected ways. What is more, even far up the Nile or in the remotest corners of the delta, the modern farmers of the Black Land have their transistor radios, and there are television sets in many villages. This has made the country people well aware of the present-day world beyond their villages.

With farmable land in such short supply, there is no room in the Black Land for pastureland for animals to graze. Animals are therefore fed on fodder crops that are cut and brought to them or are taken out to forage in the small areas of wasteland, for example, alongside irrigation canals.

A trade in food

Now that the population of Egypt has become too numerous to be fed on what can be grown on the country's own land, the Egyptians have to import more than half of the food they eat, and even more of certain basics. For example, by the late 1980s, they were having to bring in six million

tons of wheat every year, or 75 percent of their needs. Today, therefore, not only the government but also the villagers worry about market prices in parts of the world far from Egypt. Money has to be raised overseas to import all this food.

This means that the government has the difficult problem of deciding how much of the scarce farmland should be used for growing food crops directly, and how much might be better used to grow crops like cotton, that can be sold for good prices abroad. The cash they bring in can help to buy more food than the land they use up in Egypt would have grown. However, prices go up and down. Is a change in fashion for summer clothes in the United States likely to raise the price for the kind of fine cotton grown in Egypt? Do the supermarkets of Europe still want to buy the early potatoes grown on the delta? How expensive is it going to be for the Egyptians to buy North American or Australian wheat? These are the kinds of questions the Egyptians have to ask.

Imported food is costing the Egyptians several billion dollars every year, and finding enough money to pay on time is not easy. Sometimes, the countries supplying the food are unwilling to send more until they have been paid. At times France and Canada have stopped delivering grain altogether. In 1988 Egypt had to make a hasty payment of $600 million to Australia toward debts for wheat that had already been received, before the Australians would send any more.

What is actually grown on the Black Land, therefore, depends partly on changes in world markets and in government regulations. Besides cotton and potatoes, other crops grown for export

The narrow band of Black Land laid down by the river is used intensively. Even the Nile reeds are cut to make shelters and fencing; the Egyptian clover provides fodder as well as refertilizing the soil; the sugarcane is a cash crop; and the palms provide dates and fronds useful for making screens. The old boat is the kind of sailing barge used for transporting bulky cargoes such as bricks or grain.

include tobacco, vegetables such as onions, and fruits such as oranges and bananas. Sugarcane has been grown for a long time, but the export of millions of dollars' worth of strawberries is a recent development. Dates are grown all along the Nile valley. Near the towns, there is a lot of truck farming to supply the local demand for fruit and vegetables. Tomatoes are popular and, under the Egyptian sunshine, there is no need for greenhouses. Chickpeas and beans are the basis of many meals, while broad beans are used as summer food for animals, too. Cattle, sheep, and goats are also fed on alfalfa and *berseem* (Egyptian clover), green in winter and dried in summer. All these animal food or fodder crops have the valuable property of putting much-needed nitrogen back into the soil.

Water and fertilizers

No less than 99.5 percent of farmland in Egypt is irrigated, that is, watered artificially, either from the Nile or from springs, wells, and boreholes in the oases in the deserts. Wherever water is available the absence of a frosty season allows crops to be grown throughout the year. The Egyptians divide the year into three main growing seasons: *shitwi* (winter), *seifi* (summer), and *nili* (autumn). On average, two crops are taken each year from each field, and sometimes many more in truck farms. Of course, this intensive use of the soil removes nutrients from it, and fertilizers have to be added. More fertilizer is used in Egypt than in all the rest of North Africa, and the amounts applied to each acre are higher than in the United States and Europe.

The quality of the soil and the availability of water varies from place to place with the Black Land. Temperatures also tend to get higher farther south in the country. These variations mean that many different cereal crops are grown, including wheat, corn, rice, and millet. Rice needs five to seven times more irrigation water than other cereals but copes better with waterlogged or salty soils. Barley survives saltiness better than wheat but also grows in the drier areas at the limits of irrigation. Millet flourishes best in the heat of Egypt.

If irrigation is badly managed, saltiness builds up in soils and poisons plants. If too much water is applied, soil chemicals are drawn up toward the surface when the extra water is evaporated by the fierce sun. In many parts of Egypt, the sun is capable of evaporating something like 39 inches

The animal-driven, water-lifting wheel has been used for over 2,000 years. The enormous wooden cogwheels dip a vertical wheel into a little canal from the Nile, and this raises the water either in pots tied onto the wheel or in metal scoops. Many villagers cannot afford power pumps, and the metal version is an example of what is called "intermediate technology," by which developing countries bring in improvements that their people can afford.

(a meter) of water from the soil in the course of a year. Where open water is exposed to the sky, the losses are higher. In conditions as severe as these, it is hardly surprising that difficulties with soil salts are very common.

The population pressures have made increasing the irrigated area a government priority, and major programs are in progress along the Nile and at the desert oases. About 1,040,000 acres (430,000 hectares) of land have been reclaimed in the last 20 years. However, around half of this land is already unproductive because of saltiness. Since the time of the pharaohs there have been many irrigation projects, but all too often the gains have been reduced by the creation of salty crusts in the soil.

33

5

The World of the Pharaohs

Today, as in the time of the pharaohs, the boundary between the barren Red Land and the fertile Black Land is often a remarkably clear one. In many places it is possible to stand with one foot on black soil, where the river has been able to lay down its fertile mud, while the other foot is on the barren red grit of the desert.

Many of the villages of the Black Land are still built from bricks made of sun-dried Nile mud. These are cheap to put up and keep out the fierce heat, but the villages are often unsanitary and health standards in them are even worse than in the overcrowded cities.

This sharp contrast gave the ancient Egyptians a vivid feeling for the way that life and death are found side by side. The way the Nile flood brought water and fresh soil in a yearly rebirth of their land affected their whole view of life. They

believed in a life after death. Therefore, although the most spectacular features remaining from the ancient civilization are buildings, these are not the houses or even the palaces built for the living. From king to peasant, they lived in mud-brick settlements, which have long since gone. It was their gods and their dead who were housed in temples and monuments made of stone. These were intended by the Egyptians to endure forever, and it is indeed extraordinary how long their civilization lasted.

A long-lasting civilization

In prehistoric times, approximately 8,000 years ago, the tribes living along the Nile began to come together in two groupings. Those in the south comprised the kingdom of Upper Egypt, while those lower down the course of the river and in the delta in Lower Egypt were a rival kingdom. Then, a little more than 5,000 years ago (shortly before 3100 B.C.), Narmer, King of Upper Egypt, conquered Lower Egypt and united these two lands. During the next 3,000 years Egypt was ruled by more than 30 dynasties, or ruling families of kings.

Today we call the Egyptian kings "pharaohs," but this word came to us by way of Greek through Hebrew. In ancient Egyptian the original term *per-aar* actually means "the Great House." The Egyptians used this term to refer to their rulers in much the same way that today Americans or the British may say that "The White House issued a statement..." or "Buckingham Palace agreed ...," when actually referring to the President or the Queen.

The people in this photo give an idea of the size and solidity of the buildings that the ancient Egyptians erected for their gods and their dead at Thebes and elsewhere on the Nile. Little has survived of the much less substantial buildings that were the dwellings put up for the living people, whether ordinary people or pharaohs.

We are so used to the rapid changes of our twentieth-century world that it is difficult to understand what it could have been like to have lived in a civilization that flourished for 30 centuries. There were certainly dramatic events from time to time—upheavals within Egypt, wars with other great Middle Eastern empires, and fights with raiders like the Peoples of the Sea. However, to a greater extent than with most other civilizations, the way that the difficult and almost

The shaduf, or pole-and-bucket lever, has been in use in Egypt for well over 3,000 years. Instead of straining to lift a bucket full of water directly, when the bucket is empty the operator just leans on the bucket end of the lever. This force lifts the weight at the other end of the seesaw. When the bucket is full, the operator lets go and that weight swings down, lifting the bucket.

uninhabited Red Land on either side separated the ancient Egyptians from other people allowed them to carry on their same basic life-style for not just hundreds but thousands of years.

Despite all the developments and political changes of the recent past, parts of the ancient Egyptians' life-style still continue in places. Even today, some of the farming methods still in use are those developed when the pharaohs ruled. The boys and girls raising water from the Nile to their fields may be listening to Arabic pop music on a transistor radio, but some still use a *shaduf* or *sakkia*. The shaduf or pole-and-bucket lever has been used since at least the time of Tutankhamen, well over 3,000 years ago, and the sakkia, or animal-driven water-lifting wheel, was developed over 2,000 years ago.

The pyramids

The pharaohs who ruled over the united Egypt generally made their base in the central Nile valley, for example at Thebes. At Luxor and Karnak there are magnificent temples, which stand opposite the Valley of the Kings. Many of the pharaohs (including Tutankhamen) were buried in all their splendor in this valley.

However, the greatest monuments left by the ancient Egyptians are at Giza, near Cairo. The Great Pyramid there was built for Cheops (or Khufu in Egyptian), whose reign began about 2589 B.C. In ancient times, the pyramids were reckoned to be one of the Seven Wonders of the World, and even today the Cheops pyramid is still

Tutankhamen's Tomb

Today Tutankhamen has become one of the most famous of the ancient Egyptian pharaohs. However, he was actually a minor prince. He ruled from about 1354 to 1345 B.C. and died while a teenager, having achieved little to warrant his current fame.

He is famous simply because for more than 3,000 years his tomb escaped the looters, who raided the tombs in the Valley of the Kings for their treasures. Tutankhamen's tomb was discovered in 1922 by Howard Carter, working for the Earl of Carnarvon. It was intact and still contained its golden mummy cases and jewelry. Not only had it not been disturbed, but all wooden articles and other perishable materials had been preserved by the dryness of the desert. It was just as it had been left, and it gave the archaeologists an unrivaled opportunity to study the ritual ceremonies of the Egyptian cult of the dead.

The Great Sphinx and the pyramid of Kephren, a son of Cheops. Some of the covering of fine limestone slabs has survived at the top, but most of the covering of this pyramid has been looted, being used in the building of Cairo since medieval times.

the largest stone building in the Old World. It is not the largest monument ever constructed, however. The Quetzacotl pyramid in Mexico is larger, covering a greater area though it is only 177 feet (54 meters) tall. The Cheops pyramid is more than twice as high. Its original height was 481 feet (146.5 meters). Despite the loss of some stones from its top, it is still 450 feet (137 meters) tall. Each side of its base is 756 feet (1,230 meters) long, and it covers over 13 acres (5 hectares). It is estimated to contain about 2,300,000 limestone blocks, many weighing 15 tons or more.

The skills of the pyramid's builders and engineers are as impressive as its size. When archaeologists made plans of the pyramids, they found that the pharaoh's surveyors had worked

39

to high standards of accuracy. Although each of the four sides of the Cheops pyramid is more than a tenth of a mile long, they all agree in length to within eight inches (20 centimeters). The right angles at the corners of its base are equally precise; the early engineers got them correct to within a twentieth of a degree. In order to build such great structures without power tools and heavy engineering equipment, the ancient Egyptians had to be very well organized. Thousands of men were required to cut the stone blocks, bring them to the site, then drag them up great earthen ramps into place on the pyramid.

Other skills of the ancient Egyptians
Surveying, engineering, and water management were by no means the only technical skills of the ancient Egyptians. For instance, they had doctors and surgeons. Some of their treatments, based on careful observation, are still recognized as being sound and sensible by modern doctors.

We know about their medicine because they wrote about it, and about many other things in their lives. Sometimes the texts were painted or carved on walls. They were also written on papyrus, a type of paper made from reeds that grow along the Nile. The Egyptians had several kinds of writing, the most famous of which is the kind of picture writing called hieroglyphics. Hieroglyphic writing was first developed over 5,000 years ago and it remained in use until the early centuries of the Christian era. A hieroglyphic inscription found on the island of Philae in the Nile near Aswan bears a date that deciphers to August 24, A.D. 394.

The Name of Queen Cleopatra

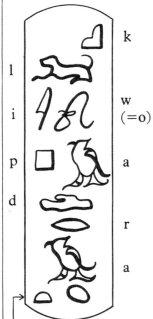

k

l

w
(=o)

i

p

a

d

r

a

The bottom two signs mean "goddess queen."

Hieroglyphic Writing

From the start, Egyptian hieroglyphs seem to have used pictures in two main ways. The first was to show directly what the writer had in mind. Thus a man could be shown simply by drawing a man. The second way was used for ideas that were difficult to suggest directly. For example, how could you show that the man was a son, rather than a brother? One way of doing this was to use puns, which are words that happen to have the same sound as what you want to indicate. If we were making up hieroglyphics for the English language, we might indicate a son by showing a man with a drawing of the sun beside him. In the Egyptian language, the word for son actually sounds like the word for a goose, so a picture of the bird was used. Sons might not have liked being shown as geese, but at least they were better off than their mothers, who were shown as vultures! It is possible to put whole sentences into picture code in this way. For example, in English, "I saw you" might be drawn as "an eye" + "a carpenter's saw" + "a female sheep (ewe)."

Toward the end of the period when hieroglyphs were used, whole words might be spelled letter by letter, using a separate picture-pun for each letter. However, writing this way took up lots of space and took time to draw or carve. More commonly the Egyptians felt they could get the meaning across without having to put in all the signs, and they tended to leave out the vowel sounds (a, e, i, o, u). This did not cause as many problems as might be expected (w-th pr-ct-c-, -t -snt d-ff-c-lt t--nd-rst-nd!) but it does mean we cannot be sure just how ancient Egyptian sounded.

The writings of the ancient Egyptians and their monuments both show that although their civilization developed in its own very special way, they were not just inward-looking people. The Nile offered a route into Africa in one direction, and toward the Middle East and Mediterranean Sea in the other. The Egyptians also sent voyagers sailing down the Red Sea. As early as the time of Queen Hatshepsut (1504-1483 B.C.), they were going far down the coast of East Africa to the mysterious land of Punt. It seems possible that a thousand years later explorers sent out by Necho II (610-595 B.C.) really did sail right around Africa. They set out down the Red Sea and came back three years later by way of Gibraltar and the Mediterranean.

6

Egyptians and Outsiders

Egyptians have always been in contact with other Middle Eastern and African peoples, in peace and in war. A wall carving made more than 3,000 years ago at Abu Simbel celebrates the victories of Ramses II by showing prisoners of war from many lands, distinguished by their different hair and beard styles.

Set apart by its red deserts, Egypt has been recognizable as a single state for the last 5,000 years. It was during what archaeologists call the New Kingdom period, over 3,000 years ago (1567-1085 B.C.), that ancient Egypt's power, wealth, and empire reached their greatest extent. This was the period of famous pharaohs like Akhenaton, Tutankhamen, Queen Hatshepsut, and the several Thutmoses and Ramses. They extended Egypt's influence both southward up the Nile into Nubia and northeastward into Asia.

Words from Ancient Egyptian

Very few words from the ancient Egyptian language have passed into use in the other languages of the world, in spite of the influence the ancient Egyptians had on their neighbors in Africa and Asia.

The ancient Egyptians called the arid land around the fertile floodplain of the Nile *d-sh-r-t*. We do not know how it was pronounced but from it we get our word desert.

A few terms that contain the names of the old gods are still used in science. There was a temple of the great god Amun out in the desert at Siwa, and the chemical found in the salt crust at the oasis there is still known as ammonia. The word oasis itself comes from the Egyptian for a cauldron, as in a big pot holding water.

Most of the words that have survived from ancient Egyptian were in fact passed on by Greeks who had come to live in Egypt. For example, the Egyptian *hbyn* was a tree with hard black wood, which grew in Nubia. The Greeks made that *ebenos,* giving us ebony. *S-aa-k* was a container that held things, from the Greek version *sakkos* we get sack.

Many of the words for things we think of as typically Egyptian are called by the names the Greeks gave to them in ancient times. Even things that seem very Egyptian, like the Nile River itself and the sphinx, get their names from Greek. Sometimes the names suggest the Greeks were more amused than impressed by the enormous monuments of the ancient civilization. Obelisk comes from *obeliskoi,* meaning spits (sharp sticks used for roasting meat), while they called the pyramids after *puramides,* little pointed cakes made out of wheat and honey!

Nubians, like this merchant in Aswan, speak a language more closely related to some East African languages than to Arabic. He is smoking a shishah (hubble-bubble), which is a water-cooled tobacco pipe.

Foreign rulers

However, by the sixth century B.C., the trend for outsiders to hold power over Egypt had started. In 525 B.C., Cambyses, the son of Persia's Cyrus the Great, made Egypt a province of the Archaemenid Empire based in what was once Persia and is now Iran. Persian influence continued almost continuously until Alexander the Great, a Greek from Macedonia, captured the Nile valley from Darius III in 332 B.C.

In his drive for world conquest, Alexander had several cities named after him, including four in what are now Turkey, Afghanistan, and Pakistan. However, his Egyptian Alexandria is where he is believed to be buried. He selected the site for the city himself, at a place he thought could be a great port and commercial center for trade between East and West. He had the city set out on a huge grid system, with the main street stretching for over four miles (seven kilometers).

Another Greek, Ptolemy, took possession of the throne after Alexander's death. He founded the Ptolemaic Dynasty of pharaohs, which ended when Cleopatra VII lost the sea battle of Actium to the Romans in 32 B.C. and she committed suicide in 30 B.C. Egypt then became part of the Roman Empire.

After Cleopatra, the Romans ruled Egypt until Roman power collapsed in the West. Then the Byzantine Empire, based in Constantinople (now Istanbul, in Turkey), took over Egypt in A.D. 395.

In A.D. 642 Alexandria was captured, and for the next two centuries Egypt's fate was closely linked with the rivalry between Arab power groups: the Ommayads based in Syria at Damascus, and the Abbasids of Baghdad in Iraq. During this period, most of the population of Egypt converted to the religion of Islam, and the Arabic language became widely adopted.

By 905 the Abbasids and Ikshidids were in power. They opposed the spread of the Shi'ia version of the faith of Islam. However, when the

The new faith of Islam sometimes took over holy sites of the ancient religion of Egypt. There is a mosque built into the temple of Amun at Luxor. During the festival celebrating the Islamic patron of the city, Sidi Abu el Haggag, a boat is carried in procession. In the times of the pharaohs, a boat also figured in ceremonies there, symbolizing the journey to the world beyond the grave.

Fatimids came to power (969-1171), this was the version of the faith that triumphed. The city of Cairo was founded during the Fatimid rule. Soon, however, Egypt was involved in fighting the Crusaders. Saladin, the great Kurdish warrior, fought the invading European Christians. On the death of the last Fatimid ruler, he also restored power to the people who followed the Sunni version of the Islamic faith. The great majority of present-day Egypt's population are Sunni Muslims. Saladin founded the Ayyubid Dynasty, which lasted from 1171 to 1252, when the Mamelukes seized power. The Arab word *memalik* means "slave," and these people had originally been slave soldiers. Various military groups, often with Turkish connections, then ruled until Egypt was conquered by the soldiers of the sultan Selim the Grim in 1517, and became part of the Ottoman Empire based in Istanbul.

Egypt remained under Ottoman control until Napoleon invaded with a French fleet and army in 1798. He took the first steps that opened up the country to European influences, which have been an important part of Egypt's recent history.

The Copts and other peoples

When foreign rulers came to Egypt they brought some of their own people with them. With the new settlers came new religions, languages, and ways of life. Egypt, like many other countries of the world, has therefore had a changing pattern of peoples over the centuries.

At the time of the Roman rule (30 B.C. to A.D. 395) there were small groups of Greeks, Jews, and Romans in the country. However, most of the people were of Egyptian origin. Some of those in the south were Nubians. Throughout the rest of the Nile valley and delta, the people were mostly the descendants of the ancient Egyptians and still spoke a version of their language. These people have come to be known as Copts. However, today the name Copt is also used for the main group of Christians in Egypt.

This confusion in the use of the word Copt shows how words and their meanings can change as they are passed from one language to another. In pre-Christian times the Egyptians had a word for the group of people descended from the ancient people of Egypt. The name meant the people of the "House of the Soul of Ptah," Ptah

A modern Coptic church in Upper Egypt.

being one of the old gods who was thought to be a creator of the world. When Arabic speakers arrived, their own letters could only imitate part of this word. Centuries later, when Europeans finally tried to put the Arabic version into the Western alphabet, what resulted was "Copt." By then, most inhabitants of Egypt had taken up

49

Islam and become speakers of Arabic. To both the Arabs and the Europeans, the term Copt had come to be associated with those Egyptians who had become Christians when the ancient gods had fallen from favor, but who had not been converted to the new religion of Islam.

Today, the Copts make up one of the largest Christian minorities in the Middle East. There are perhaps six million Copts in Egypt, but in this century many have moved to settle elsewhere because of tension between the communities in their native country. There are, for example, about 100,000 Copts now living in the United States. The Coptic language fell out of common use by the thirteenth century and Egyptian Copts now speak Arabic, but until very recently they used the old language in their church services. In this way, the Copts carried on the use of a last version of the language of the pharaohs right into the twentieth century.

Muslims and the Arabic language

The Christian Copts form a unique part of the Egyptian nation, but today nine out of ten Egyptians are Muslims. Their religion, Islam, centers on the life of the prophet Muhammad, who lived in Arabia between the Red Sea and the Arabian Gulf, from about A.D. 571 to 632. His followers spread the faith with extraordinary speed both eastward in the Middle East and westward right through North Africa and into Spain.

The spread of the Arabic language is closely related to the spread of the religion of Islam. Arabic was the language that the Prophet

The Sultan Hassan mosque, set under the walls of the Citadel of Old Cairo, is typical of the simple dignity of the architecture of many Egyptian mosques.

Muhammad spoke. Muslims believe that the Koran, their holy book, records the very words of God, so the book itself and the language in which it is written is considered sacred. Muslims believe it cannot be properly translated, and see it as part of their faith to know the Koran in its original form. Arabic as used in everyday speech has undergone some changes in parts of the large area where it is spoken, but even so, Egyptians who want to work abroad find no language barrier throughout the Arabic-speaking countries of the Middle East and North Africa.

7 Egypt's Recent History

Napoleon and the French saw the importance of Egypt as a stepping-stone for European powers on the route to their empires in India and beyond. However, so did Britain. The French arrived in Egypt in 1798, but later the same year the British navy, under Lord Nelson, won the Battle of the Nile. At this battle the French fleet was destroyed, and this defeat led ultimately to the

Napoleon's basic reason for taking an army to Egypt was to develop France's colonial empire in rivalry to Britain. Here in a nineteenth-century illustration he is shown presenting an Egyptian sheik with a sash in the form of the French flag.

downfall of the French occupation of Egypt in 1801 after only three years.

When Napoleon was forced to admit defeat, the Turkish Sultan appointed Muhammad Ali (an army officer from Macedonia) as ruler. The Mamelukes were eager to regain power, but Muhammad Ali rid himself of his Mameluk rivals by inviting 300 of them to a banquet in Cairo and murdering them. By 1805 Ali was undisputed ruler of Egypt, determined to modernize the country and create a powerful independent state. His dynasty remained the official rulers of Egypt until the Revolution of 1952.

European influences
The construction of the Suez Canal, connecting the Red Sea to the Mediterranean, confirmed the international importance of Egypt. The canal took

---

Earlier Canals
The Suez Canal is not a new idea. A canal linking the Nile to the Red Sea was actually dug in the time of the Pharaoh Necho (610-595 B.C.). Herodotus says it took four days to pass through it, though two warships could go side by side. By the time of the Persian invasion of Egypt in the sixth century B.C. it had filled up with sand from the desert, but Darius I had it cleaned out about 518 B.C. The canal became clogged up yet again, but was reopened for a while by the Ptolemys in Roman times. When de Lesseps finished the canal connecting the Red Sea directly to the Mediterranean, instead of to the Nile, he also rebuilt the ancient waterway so that villagers on its route could get fresh water from the Nile again.

ten years to dig and was completed in 1869 by Ferdinand de Lesseps. It was 108 miles (173 kilometers) long and originally 24 feet (7.3 meters) deep. The canal meant ships did not have to go all the way around Africa when traveling between North American or European ports and India or Australia. It quickly became a vital link in both commercial and naval movements around the world. The European powers were anxious that this link should not be endangered, and in 1882 after a series of political and financial crises British forces moved into Egypt.

The Turkish rulers remained in place, but in effect British officials ran many aspects of the country until the 1920s. This arrangement worked well in many practical respects, but after so many centuries of dominance by outsiders,

One of the legacies of the British era in Egypt is the national museum building. Although this building houses the treasures of the pharaohs, in style it looks as though it belongs more in England than in a Middle Eastern country.

From Victorian times right through World Wars I and II until the 1950s, British servicemen were part of the Egyptian scene.

In the Fish-Market.

many Egyptians were eager to gain their independence. Led by Saad Zaghlul Pasha, the father of Egyptian nationalism, they became mostly independent in 1922. However, British influence remained strong, and during World War II (1939-1945) Egypt was a vital base for the fight against the forces of Mussolini and Hitler in North Africa and the Middle East.

This long association with the British and the involvement of Egypt in World Wars I and II are parts of the country's history that have affected its economic development up to the present day. Many of the countries of the Middle East have very little history of industrial development. In some cases, right up until the present oil era, no real industries existed. Most goods were made by hand in small workshops. In Egypt, on the other hand, industry has been developing all through this century. World Wars I and II helped this process. The difficulty of getting supplies out to the Middle East in wartime meant that the British encouraged the development of a wide range of manufacturing in Egypt. However, today many of the factories are old-fashioned and inefficient. Finding money to modernize them is now one of Egypt's problems.

Egypt between World War II and 1970

The time since World War II has not been very settled or easy for the Egyptians. In 1948, along with four other Arab nations, Egypt took part in the war in Palestine when the Jewish state of Israel was proclaimed. Palestine is the traditional name for part of the land along the eastern coast of the Mediterranean. When the new Jewish state was first created there, and then later extended by Israeli occupation of neighboring areas, many Palestinian Arabs left as refugees. Others found that they had to live under a government with which they disagreed. As a leading Arab state, Egypt has been deeply involved in the problems of this region.

In 1952, Colonel Gamal Abdul Nasser seized power from Farouk, the King of Egypt, and the following year Egypt was declared a republic. In 1956 Colonel Nasser took full control of the Suez Canal for Egypt. In response British and French troops seized the Canal Zone, and the Israelis attacked through the Sinai Peninsula. Pressure from both the United States and the Soviet Union forced the British and French to withdraw. The

United States government refused aid for the construction of the Aswan High Dam, but the Soviet Union agreed to finance the project, thereby extending its influence in the Middle East. Egypt also accepted military equipment from the Soviet Union to use against the Israelis, who were equipped with weapons from the United States and France.

In 1958 Egypt and Syria together called themselves "The United Arab Republic," but too many of their interests clashed and they parted again in 1961. Tension between the Egyptians and the Israelis grew, and war broke out in 1967. In six days Egypt lost its lands on the Sinai Peninsula as far as the Suez Canal. Following this war, relations between Egypt and the Soviet Union became closer. There was further trouble between Israel and Egypt in 1969, and then in 1970 Egypt's President Nasser died suddenly.

Egypt since 1970
Nasser was succeeded by President Anwar al Sadat. Faced by Egypt's serious difficulties in paying for its needs, Sadat began to encourage more private enterprise in business. In 1972 he expelled the Soviets from Egypt. Then, shortly after further fighting with Israel in 1973, he returned to friendly relations with the United States. In 1975 he signed a peace agreement with Israel. This displeased many of the other Arab states of the Middle East, but it was the Egyptians who had been bearing the main burden of the troubles with Israel for a long time. Egypt had suffered badly both directly in the fighting and in the cost of the country's economy. Part of this cost

Deepening the Suez Canal
Before the Suez Canal was closed by the 1967 war, eight major recuttings had increased its depth to 38 feet (11.6 meters). While it was closed, many larger oil tankers were built and general cargo ships also increased in size. After the canal was reopened in 1975, a billion dollars was spent to increase its depth to 53 feet (16.2 meters), to take ships of up to 150,000 tons. This was to ensure that the canal recaptured a good share of world trade.

Now about seven percent of the whole world's seaborne trade goes through the canal. About 40 percent by volume of the goods taken along the canal are oil or oil products. Different regions depend on the canal to different extents. Thus, while Australia and New Zealand do not use it much, nearly a third of all goods imported into the Mediterranean pass that way. Often between 50 and 60 ships go through each day. The maximum speed allowed is just 8.7 miles per hour (14 kph) so as not to erode the banks, and it takes a day for a ship to make the passage.

was due to the loss of much-needed income from foreign ships using the Suez Canal, which had become blocked during the 1967 fighting. With the help of British divers, the canal was reopened in 1975.

In 1979 Israel returned the Sinai Peninsula to Egypt following an agreement made the previous year at Camp David, Maryland, between Sadat and Menachem Begin, the Israeli leader. The United States promised major financial aid to help rebuild Egypt's economy, which had been

The sheer number of mosques in old Cairo is a reminder of the continuing importance of religion as a factor in present-day Egyptian politics.

damaged by the 30 years of stress with Israel. In spite of his successes, Sadat had upset several groups in Egypt with his political, religious, and economic policies. There were riots, and then in 1981 he was killed by extremists.

During the 1980s, life did not get easier for the Egyptians. The country is a democratic socialist

59

state, with a National Assembly of two houses (a People's Assembly and a Consultative Council). This two-house system of government is not unlike that of the United States and, as in the United States, a great deal depends on the character of the elected president. During the 1980s the leading figure was President Hosni Mubarak, who had to face serious problems. Violence within Egypt has underlined the difficulty of leading a country where the government's policies can be regarded as being either "too liberal" or "too strict" by rival groups of extremists.

On top of these problems at home, Egypt's relationship with other countries, whether neighbors or superpowers, are also complicated. There have been serious disagreements with Libya and Syria, as well as difficulties with the different organizations that support the Palestinian Arabs in their struggles with the state of Israel. Egypt has tried also not to become too dependent on either of the superpowers. By the late 1980s, more than $2 billion of aid was being accepted each year from the United States, but contacts with the Soviet Union had also been increased after normal diplomatic relations were restored with them in 1985. Egypt has also been building up more links with individual European countries, such as Italy, to offset the influence of the superpowers.

8 Development and Industry

Even in ancient times, the population of the land of the pharaohs was already large enough to be reaching the limits of what the Black Land could support. If over some years the Nile flood failed to rise to its usual level, not enough food could be grown and people starved.

Toward the end of the period of the pharaohs, when the Romans took over, there were perhaps 8 million people living in Egypt. After all the troubled history that followed, the population fell and it may have been as low as 2.5 million at the start of the nineteenth century, when Napoleon

The population of Egypt has increased rapidly in the last 50 years, rising from 15 million in 1936 to over 50 million today. Cairo is one of the world's largest and most crowded cities.

was there. However, during the nineteenth century the number of people began to increase rapidly, and by the beginning of the twentieth century the population had reached 10 million. The speed of the population growth has increased ever since. By 1936 the population had reached 15 million, and it doubled to over 30 million by 1966. The 50 million mark was passed by 1986, and it is estimated that the population may reach 70 million by 2000.

Increasing demands
It is unlikely that Egypt will ever again be able to grow enough food for all its people, despite attempts to increase the cultivated areas. More and more foodstuffs will have to be imported. The increasing population also needs more and more housing, power and water supply, sewage disposal, and so forth, as well as medical facilities, other social services, and education. Egypt has to find money to meet these needs. At the same time as the demand is increasing because of the sheer number of people, the ambitions of the Egyptians for a better standard of living are rising. People want to have all kinds of consumer goods. Several million Egyptians have now had the experience of working abroad in oil-rich countries and have seen the life-styles enjoyed by some of the people there. In normal times the citizens of states such as Saudi Arabia, Kuwait, and the United Arab Emirates have average annual incomes higher than those of the United States or Switzerland. Even Egyptians who have stayed at home in little villages along the Nile are now conscious of the television

images of the life-styles of rich people. Thus there is pressure on Egypt to import not only basic necessities, but luxury goods, too.

The result has been that Egypt has what is called a serious balance of trade deficit. In other words, what is imported to Egypt tends to cost a great deal more than what the country is able to export and sell abroad. Egypt gets most of its imports from the United States, Germany, France, Italy, and Japan. Its exports go particularly to Italy, the Soviet Union, Britain, Czechoslovakia, West Germany, and Greece. The Egyptian debt now totals billions of dollars each year. Many countries have become unwilling to lend money to Egypt, or to send goods on credit, because they are worried about whether and when they will receive their money.

Industrial pollution is now a serious problem in Cairo. The smog catches in one's throat and often makes it difficult to see the pyramids at Giza. However, just a short distance away from the city the desert air may be crystal clear.

Unfortunately, by making it difficult for the Egyptians to borrow money to build new factories, Egypt has been unable to improve its own industry at home. Manufacturing more goods for themselves would be one way of cutting down on expensive imports. Many existing Egyptian factories were built in the first half of the twentieth century and are now old-fashioned and inefficient. Many large state-run enterprises are only working at a half or sometimes even a third of their capacity. Often they employ many more people than competing factories in other countries, and this means their goods cost more to make. In recent years, medium- and small-sized privately run firms have done better than the national businesses, and government has encouraged them.

Much of Egyptian industry is based on agricultural products. Cane sugar has been refined by the Arabs for hundreds of years. It has been an important commercial product in Egypt throughout this century, and now 75 percent of the sugar output of the whole Middle East is grown there. Here a narrow-gauge railroad is being used to transport the crop between plantation and factory.

A variety of industries

Many of the industries now found in Egypt resulted from the cultivation of the Black Land. Some of these industries involve the processing of food, including crops such as sugarcane. Textile industries, based on crops such as cotton, have also developed. Other Egyptian industries reflect the needs of the farmers. For example, there are major plants developing fertilizer at Talkha and Abu Qir.

Egypt's Cotton Industry
Cotton textile manufacturing has long been the largest single industrial activity in Egypt, employing over 33 percent of all the people working in industry, and producing 25 percent of Egypt's total industrial output. At a time when the world cotton trade has had difficulties with competition from cheap artificial materials, Egypt has been able to keep its industry going by specializing in growing long-fiber cottons. These can be spun into silky threads for high-quality garments.

In the busy market streets of Egypt many vendors have stands selling textiles made from cotton grown in Egypt. Egypt specializes in fine cotton suitable for high-quality clothing.

Industries based on Egypt's mineral resources include some aluminum processing at Nag Hammadi, near Qena. Iron processing is mainly based at Helwan, near Cairo. At Helwan there are also vast cement works, helping to supply the enormous demand for construction materials for the rapidly growing city of Cairo.

Much of the manufacturing industry of Egypt is in fact centered in Cairo itself. The agriculturally based industries are certainly represented there in food processing, brewing, leather working, and textiles. There is also cement making and the manufacture of chemicals, plus an extraordinary range of small factories making everything from furniture to tourist souvenirs or perfume. Some of the high-technology industries of Egypt, such as electronics, are located in the city, and there is an advanced pharmaceutical industry making medicines. Egypt is unique in the Arab world, for it produces 80 percent of the medical drugs it needs.

The requirements of two world wars and the fighting with Israel have led to the development of a light metal goods industry in both Cairo and Alexandria. Car assembly is another important industry in Alexandria, which has also become a major center for oil refining and natural gas processing.

The power industries
Egypt's oil and gas reserves provide some of the power needed for industry as well as for the fast-increasing domestic demand. Some Middle Eastern countries have enough oil reserves to last

them far into the future, but Egyptian reserves are much more limited. Most of the Egyptian oil production is concentrated around the Gulf of Suez on the Red Sea, and in the Sinai fields returned by Israel. Oil and, increasingly, natural gas are also now being exploited in the Western Desert. At present, oil exports help bring in the money that Egypt so desperately needs to pay for its food and other imports. However, unless really big new finds are made, at present rates of consumption Egypt's reserves will be running low by the end of this century. Not only will there be none extra to sell, but Egypt will need to import oil to have enough for its own use.

Egypt is not rich in other power resources, such as coal. However, for power production, as in so many other ways, the Nile is of special

The Aswan High Dam is so big that it forms the entire horizon of this photo. In the foreground is one of the great halls which hold the turbines that generate the hydroelectric power as water is released from Lake Nasser behind the dam.

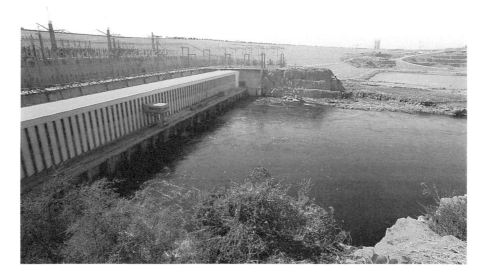

importance to Egypt. From the start, the Aswan High Dam was planned as a source of hydroelectric power as well as of water for irrigation. In some years the great turbines built into the dam have in fact generated more than 50 percent of the electricity produced in Egypt, although 20 percent is more usual. However, there are problems.

For one thing, although the amount of electric power needed for industry is much the same throughout the year, the demand for water for irrigating crops varies with the seasons. This fact means that it is hard to make the best use of the water for generating power. When droughts in central Africa lower the level of Lake Nasser, difficult decisions have to be made about cutting the electricity supply. Another problem is the fact that the dam generates its electricity in the south of Egypt, whereas the great majority of the people and the industries needing that power are in the north, between 430-560 miles (700-900 kilometers) away. A lot of power is lost in sending electricity along transmission lines stretching all the way from Aswan to Cairo and Alexandria.

9

Cities, Towns, and Transportation

Cairo is a city of contrasts. In the foreground is Gezirah, an island in the Nile with spacious recreation facilities. On the facing riverbank stand international tourist hotels along the fashionable Corniche. Then the haze of pollution thickens over tightly packed old Cairo with its markets, workshops, and slums.

Cairo dominates Egypt today. It is not only the largest city and the capital of the country, it is by far the largest city in all Africa, and indeed around the Mediterranean. Cairo has become much bigger than many famous cities of the United States, or Europe. Nobody is quite sure how many people now live in the built-up area of Cairo. The city has outgrown its official boundaries, engulfed nearby smaller towns, and spread across the Nile to Giza. Depending on where the count is stopped, there are certainly at least 10 million and perhaps 15 million people in

the built-up area. It is still spreading fast, and some estimates suggest it will have 17 million people by the end of the twentieth century.

Egypt's other main city is Alexandria, on the coast. This was Egypt's first great city, started by the Greek ruler Alexander the Great in the fourth century B.C. During Roman times the city had a population of over one million people, including slaves. However, by the early nineteenth century, at the time Napoleon arrived, this once-great Mediterranean port had declined to a collection of ruins around its clogged harbor. It began to revive as a commercial port soon afterward, when it was joined to the Nile by a canal. Since then it has benefited both from its position as the seaport connecting the rapidly developing Cairo to the world's oceans and from the creation of the Suez Canal. All this trade has helped it to become an industrial center in its own right. Like Cairo, it has been growing spectacularly and now around one in ten Egyptians lives there.

Cairo

The city of Cairo developed at the junction of the two main inhabited regions of Egypt, the narrow river valley and the broad lands of the delta; nearby is the big, productive Fayyum Oasis. Cairo is well placed to be the distributing and marketing center for all of Egypt. Most of the food grown in the delta is marketed there. Since the time of the pharaohs, the Nile has offered a north-south route through the deserts, between the Mediterranean and the interior of Africa. Cairo developed where a natural east-west land route between the Middle East and North Africa crosses the north-south river route. The city is sited where an island offers a stepping-stone across the Nile.

Control of this position has been valued by most rulers of Egypt. Cairo became the center of power and government, with the influence and employment which that gives. Today the city can offer jobs in the civil service as well as employment in the head offices of banks and commercial companies. Cairo is also Egypt's educational center, with several universities, and the center of publishing. Many newspapers have daily circulations of half a million copies.

All these jobs, in manufacturing and service industries, commerce and administration have drawn people to Cairo from all over the rest of Egypt. It has seemed a place of opportunity for people of every level of education, from university graduates seeking to advance their careers in electronics to laborers who see a chance of regular work in the city's endless building sites. The movement of so many people into the city during the last 50 years or so has given it a particular pattern of settlement. People have naturally tended to head for districts of the city where relatives or friends from their own towns or villages had already settled. Thus, there are distinct neighborhoods where many of the people will have come originally from a particular town up the Nile, like Asyut or Idfu, or neighborhoods of Nubians who have had to move from the lands drowned by Lake Nasser.

Part of the great growth of Cairo in the twentieth century is due to this influx of people from elsewhere in Egypt. However, it is also due in part to improvements in the city's hospital services, in sewage control, and in basic hygiene. Safer drinking water and better diets have also helped to ensure that fewer people die of diseases, leading to rapid population growth.

The sheer rate at which Cairo is expanding means, however, that there is a constant struggle with such matters as sewage disposal and electricity supply. There are also serious air pollution problems, and it is sometimes difficult to see the pyramids across the Nile through the smog. Road congestion can be very bad despite a modernized suburban railway system and new highways. The traffic accident rate in Cairo is among the worst in the world, more than 16 times that of New York or ten times that of London. Over 1,000 people are killed on the city's roads in some years. During the rush hour, people can be seen hanging onto the outside of overcrowded buses and trains. The bus service carries more than three million passengers each day. Above all, despite continual construction activity, there are never enough houses. So many people are crowded into parts of Cairo that the population density is greater than in New York or Tokyo.

It is a measure of the overcrowding that in recent times well over half a million of Cairo's people have been living as squatters in the city's sprawling burial grounds. In the City of the Dead, a cemetery on the eastern side of Cairo, many of the tombs are in the form of little buildings. Whole families have moved in and now live in these. The television aerials above some of the tombs show that it is not only the poorest of the poor who are unable to find better places to live.

Other settlements

Sheer size and rate of growth set present-day Alexandria and Cairo apart from the rest of Egypt. Most of the other towns are much smaller. They often have a rural air because many are essentially market towns serving the large proportion of Egypt's population who still get their living directly by farming the Black Land. The towns that are the main exceptions to this are also generally quite small. Port Said, Ismailiya, and Suez itself serve the Suez Canal. Then there are the industrial towns like Helwan, and tourist resorts. The older centers are at the ancient monuments on the Nile, but others are springing up to offer water sports along the Red Sea coast. Although very small, these tourist towns are important to Egypt because of the amount of foreign money they bring into the country.

Many of the farmers' villages along the Nile are tiny, because of the narrowness of the strip of Black Land throughout much of the valley. However, in the great plain of the delta, there is a different pattern. There, farming settlements of more than 10,000 people can be found. In spite of their size, these are perhaps best regarded as giant villages rather than as actual towns. They lack many of the facilities and services found in most towns and are essentially just the homes of peasant farming families. They have grown so large because the Black Land of the delta is so fertile and well watered that in places it can support over 5,200 people per square mile (over 2,000 per square kilometer). Thus 10,000 people can live in a single settlement and yet be within easy walking distance of the fields they farm.

Transportation

It is still an adventure to take an expedition into some of the rugged and empty Red Land areas of the Western Desert and Eastern Highlands. However, all the towns and the main oases of Egypt are well served by transportation links. There are aircraft flights between the main settlements of the country, and also to places of special interest to tourists. The almost 11,200 miles (18,000 kilometers) of surfaced roads include freight links from Cairo to Alexandria, to the Suez Canal, to the Fayyum Oasis, and to the towns up the Nile all the way to Aswan. There are frequent bus services over this road network. There are also almost 2,200 miles (3,500 kilometers) of railroads, with express trains from Cairo to Alexandria and up the Nile to Aswan.

This photo shows part of the central bus station in Cairo, in a haze of diesel exhaust. City buses move over three million commuters each day. They are inexpensive but often overcrowded.

The high triangular sails of the Nile felluccas are well designed for catching the gentle breezes that come over the cliffs and palm trees which often line the riverbanks. The villagers still use boats as the cheapest form of travel.

Since the time of the pharaohs boats have been important for transporting both people and cargo along the Nile. The south-to-north flow of the river carries heavily loaded barges downstream, then the reliable north-to-south winds allow them to be sailed back against the current. Even today, sails are still used on the boats known as *felluccas*. Market towns and the villages between them are regularly linked by felluccas.

Even the enlarged Suez Canal is not really large enough to take all the big oil tankers, so the Egyptians have now built an overland Suez-Mediterranean pipeline (the SUMED). This pipeline can handle around the same volume of oil as goes through the canal by ship, thus helping to keep up the country's earnings.

75

10 Problems and Solutions

The rate at which the population is increasing is likely to remain Egypt's main problem in the foreseeable future. In several other Middle Eastern countries the population is also increasing quickly. However, although this is creating problems for them too, most of these other countries either have more oil or less severe limits on their area of farmable land than Egypt. The rate of population growth in Egypt has been getting faster and faster throughout this century. This is almost entirely the result of natural increase within the country, since few people come from elsewhere to settle in Egypt.

Birth and death rates

In Islamic countries, with their strong emphasis on family life, almost everybody expects to marry early and have many children. Traditionally, a large number of relatives is seen as an advantage. They can help each other in difficult times, and parents feel that they will not be abandoned in their old age. In Egypt, until recently, most mothers tended to have around seven children, and despite attempts by the government to encourage smaller families, the average is still over five. Those couples wanting fewer children tend to be among the better-off people, well-educated and ambitious to get good jobs.

If a country with limited natural resources like Egypt is to be able to earn what it needs in the

About 40 percent of the entire Egyptian population is like this boy less than 15 years old.

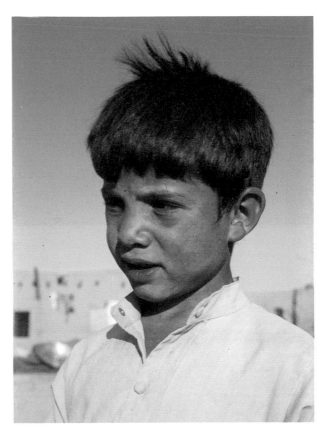

high-technology world of the late twentieth century, it is clearly vital that the population become well educated. There are now enough secondary school places for about half the children. However, it is very difficult to build enough schools and train enough teachers to keep pace with the high birthrate. Well over a million children are now being added to the Egyptian population each year. That is much more than the entire population of some other

77

For some diseases the death rate is five times higher in country areas than in Egypt's cities. Not only do cities tend to have better medical care, but many diseases are waterborne, and working with irrigation water and living beside canals can be unhealthy. Living in mud-brick huts in close proximity to livestock also spreads disease and parasites.

Middle Eastern states, such as Qatar or Bahrain. Today, four out of ten Egyptians are under the age of 15. Not only do they need education, but they also place a financial burden on the small number of working grown-ups. Their earnings and taxes have to pay for all these young people.

It seems very likely that the numbers of schoolchildren will increase even more, as medical standards continue to improve. At present, one baby in ten still dies. The losses are particularly high in the rural areas, where living conditions in the mud-brick villages are poorer and medical care is less effective than it has become in the cities with their modern hospitals.

There are still problems for infants, but Egyptian people now have a much better chance of living through their childhood and adult years

than in the past. Even in 1950, the average life expectancy was just 42 years, compared to over 70 in the United States, the United Kingdom, or Australia. Today, out of each 1,000 people, only about ten die each year. Just 50 years ago, Egyptian death rates were three times that and were among the highest in the world. It is this remarkable decline in death rates that has been largely responsible for the population increase. Death rates could be reduced still further, and since the birth rate seems likely to remain quite high, it is unlikely that there will be a sudden slowing of the growth rate.

Controlling disease
Until the nineteenth century, Cairo, like many of the other cities of the Middle East, was regarded as something of a death trap. Poor hygiene and crowded conditions led to epidemics of diseases like cholera, typhoid, and even bubonic plague. Successful efforts to improve hygiene and medical services led to less disease, and Egypt's cities became healthier.

Conditions outside the cities were more difficult to improve. Even 50 years ago, a lot of the country people had short and miserably disease-ridden lives. Many of the diseases commonest in Egypt thrive in hot, wet environments, and the fellahin working close to their irrigation ditches are very vulnerable to them. Trachoma produces blindness. Malaria (carried by water-breeding mosquitos), bilharzia (carried by the water snails), and other waterborne parasites, such as hookworm, all lower people's resistance to killer diseases of the lungs, heart, and liver.

Contaminated water also spreads bacterial infections. There were serious epidemics right up until 1947, a year when over 20,000 people died.

Resistance to disease was also low because of poor diet. Even in the 1950s, four out of five people had a diet low in nutritious foods and vitamins. Things have improved, with increasing consumption of vegetables, dates, and melons, together with more cheese, fish, and meat.

Poor housing also harms health. During the 1980s, many new up-to-date homes were built, even in the Nile villages. These were often paid for from the high wages earned by men who had gone to work in the oil-rich states of the Middle East. However, many villagers still live in huts built of sun-dried mud bricks. Often they have only one or two dark rooms, sometimes shared

As the housing for the increasing population spreads across the Black Land, it reduces the area available for agriculture at a time when more and more food is needed.

with their animals. The shortage of space on the valuable Black Land means the huts are often crowded closely together, with narrow unhygienic alleys between them. Some of the smaller villages are still among the most unhealthy in the world. However, a major effort to bring safe, piped drinking water to every village has helped greatly in controlling disease.

Although many country people are leaving to settle in the cities, the population explosion in Egypt is becoming so great that it has been estimated that the country areas may well have to absorb at least another 15 million people by the end of the twentieth century. That is as much as the present population of the whole Cairo area. With so little extra land, and the need to improve the living standards of the country people already there, this will be extremely difficult.

Shortages of land and other resources
The growth of the towns and cities is helping to absorb people who cannot find jobs in the farming communities, but it is also making things worse by eating up good agricultural land. Suburbs are spreading over the Black Land, and great quantities of Nile mud are being used for brick making. This matters more now that the Aswan High Dam prevents a fresh supply of fertile mud from arriving each year. In an attempt to relieve the pressure along the Nile, new towns are being created, such as Sadat City, Tenth of Ramadan City, and King Khaled City.

The severe limits on the natural resources of Egypt mean that the best prospects for the country's future would seem to lie in the skills of

Education and Jobs for Women
In Egypt more women work as teachers and doctors, as well as in office jobs, than in many other Middle Eastern countries. However, in Egypt as elsewhere in the Middle East, many Muslim households feel that taking care of the family is the proper career for women. Even when this is not the case, opportunities for women are often limited in practical terms. In the 1980s, only half of Egypt's girls were completing primary education, compared with nine out of ten boys.

its people. With their long tradition of fine universities, the Egyptians have a good reputation throughout the Arabic-speaking world as teachers, doctors, lawyers, and technicians.

Highly trained Egyptians are still valued abroad at times when falling oil prices mean the end of overseas jobs for less-skilled Egyptian manual workers. However, it is difficult for the government to decide whether it is better to encourage these people to go abroad for the value of taxes on their earnings or to remain at home and use their skills in their own country. On the one hand, the Egyptians desperately need to earn foreign currency to pay for necessities like food. On the other hand, the country needs every doctor, teacher, and technician that it can train.

11 Egyptian Life Today

Young people growing up in Egypt today cannot help but be struck by the contrasts in their country. These contrasts include the contrasts between rich and poor, between the fertile farmed land and the deserts, and between the peacefulness of village life and the bustle of the cities. Young Egyptians are also very aware of the importance of Egypt in the Middle East. Other states may have much more oil, but Egypt has by far the largest population of any of the Arabic-speaking states. Its size gives Egypt great political importance in the region, with the disadvantages as well as the advantages this brings.

It is difficult to grow up in Egypt without a sense of history and an awareness of the important place of ancient Egypt in the history of world civilization. Besides the massive temple sites that tourists come to see, like those at Luxor, Karnak, or Sakkara, many smaller ruins abound. Behind many villages there are cliffs with the remains of ancient tombs, where the children play. Some of the traditional methods of raising water from the river and of farming the land also keep history alive.

Young Egyptians are very conscious of the value of the tourist trade that their history brings, with the possibility of jobs for them at all levels. Those who do well at school may learn foreign languages, and get well-paying jobs in Egypt's international banks and tourist hotels. Others may get jobs as service staff in the restaurants, hotels, and on tour boats, where tourists may pay

In Egypt, the tourists' excursion boats are known to the people of even the remotest parts of the Nile and are a constant reminder that there are other ways of earning a living besides working the land.

as much for a drink as a local laborer gets for a day's work in the fields or on a building site. Worries about Middle Eastern wars and hostage-taking may frighten away tourists in some years, but often well over a million of them come to Egypt, bringing a lot of money into the country. The government hopes that during the 1990s earnings from tourism will match those from oil.

The Muslim way of life
At school Egyptian Muslim children are taught about their religion, as well as being taught to read and write Arabic and to do arithmetic. Many make a very serious study of the Koran, Islam's holy book. Some gain great respect by learning all of it by heart.

As throughout the Muslim world, the Egyptians pray individually five times each day, and on Fridays meet for prayers in the mosques. The mosques in the villages are usually small but dignified buildings. The major mosques in Cairo, such as those of Amur, Kait Bey, or al Azhar, are among the great religious buildings of the world. It is the ambition of all Muslims to go at least once in their lifetime to Saudi Arabia to visit Mecca, the holiest place in Islam. It is not just the rich who manage a pilgrimage. Even in remote villages far up the Nile, there are poor men whose names include the title *Hadji*. This title means they have made the *Hadj*, the pilgrimage to Mecca. Most Egyptians are Sunni Muslims, the largest group of Muslims in the Middle East, but other variations of the Muslim faith are also followed.

The main feature of the Islamic year in Egypt, as elsewhere, is the holy month of Ramadan. It is both a solemn demonstration of obedience to Allah and a way of strengthening the bonds between families and friends. During Ramadan, all Muslims refrain from eating and drinking from sunrise to sunset. A meal called *iftar* is taken after the sun goes down. Iftar often starts with soup followed by eggs mixed into black beans and ends with sweets and *kamar-eldin*, a drink made from apricots. The meal is a good time for meeting friends and relatives. They spend the evening listening to Arabic music and readings from the Koran on the radio and go together to their mosque. The streets are lit up, and restaurants stay open. A second meal is taken before dawn comes, to give people stamina for fasting through the long, hot day to come.

Finding work

One reason for leaving home in Egypt is to go on pilgrimage to Mecca. Another is to find a better job, or indeed any work at all. Although agriculture in Egypt is very productive, it is seldom as highly mechanized as in North America or Europe. Oxen, buffalo, or camels are still commonly used to provide power. Often Egyptian farming seems more like truck farming, with men, women, and children working by hand using simple tools.

In spite of this intensive use of people, the increase in population means that laborers without their own land often lack work. When world oil prices are good, several million may find jobs in the oil-rich countries. They may also go to other countries where there are labor shortages due to those countries' own people having left for the oil states. Large numbers of Egyptians have worked on farms in Jordan, to replace Jordanians who had gone elsewhere to work.

When times are good, these overseas workers can send back wages worth many times what they could have earned at home. This money allows their families to build new homes and to buy up-to-date electrical household goods. However, this money from overseas work can suddenly stop. Whenever world oil prices fall, foreign workers like the Egyptians are the first to lose their jobs.

A move from the countryside to the big cities within Egypt itself does not necessarily offer an easier solution for those in need of work. There are many good jobs in Cairo and Alexandria, particularly for well-qualified people. However,

To make ends meet many people have to work long hours at several part-time jobs because of the shortage of well-paying jobs, particularly for the unskilled.

for those who have had little opportunity to gain skills it can be very difficult to find any regular work in the cities. Many people have to make a living without steady jobs. They may sell newspapers at corners to passing cars or act as porters for street traders. Often they have to do several things, because no single job earns enough to support them. This part-time, irregular work makes it difficult to judge how many Egyptians should be counted as unemployed, but it has been estimated that it might be as much as 20 or 25 percent of the work force.

With so many poor people, it is important that the Egyptian government hold down the prices of basics such as food, clothing, electricity, and public transportation. Much of Egypt's tax money is used to keep down the prices or subsidize these basics. However, this makes foreign banks and the International Monetary Fund unwilling to give Egypt much-needed loans. When attempts have been made to reduce subsidies, there has been serious rioting.

Food and clothing

It is another of the contrasts characteristic of Egypt that, despite the basic worries about growing and importing enough food and about unhealthy diets, the Egyptian style of cooking is famous throughout the Middle East. There are hundreds of dishes: spicy chicken soup made with green vegetables and garlic; fried balls of ground black beans, mixed with spices; salads of cucumbers, tomatoes, watercress, parsley, peppers, and mint; pigeon baked with rice and milk; chopped lamb with grape leaves and zucchini served with yogurt; a pumpkin dessert with nuts and vanilla sauce; *Om Ali* ("Ali's mother," named after an Egyptian Mameluk queen), a raisin cake soaked in milk, and so on. In spite of the glories of traditional Egyptian cooking, Western-style food is becoming fashionable too, at least among the well-to-do.

Western-style clothing is more often seen in Egypt, particularly in Cairo and Alexandria, than in some other Arab countries. However, many women strictly follow the traditions of Islamic dress. For men, the characteristic loose gown of the Middle East and North Africa is favored as a very practical garment in the heat. The headgear in Egypt is often a scarf wound around the head, rather than the more usual Arab headcloth.

Broadcasting in Egypt

When he set up the Republic of Egypt, Colonel Nasser decided that radio and television broadcasting could offer an effective way of influencing how people thought and politically bonding the new state of Egypt together. He started a state-run television service in 1961, the first of its kind in Africa. The service offers two channels, the main one being relayed all over Egypt. The other channel covers the Cairo/Alexandria area. Half of the population and most of the 4.5 to 5 million television sets are in this area. There are probably over ten million radio receivers in Egypt, and these are catered to by over a dozen radio stations.

More people are employed in broadcasting in Egypt than in all the other African and Arab countries put together. The channels broadcast 20 hours a day. Since the 1970s, the programs have become less political and have turned more to entertainment. There are Egyptian soap operas, crime thrillers with plenty of car chases, and slapstick comedians. However, the fact that Egypt is an Islamic country is not neglected. At the times of day set aside for prayer, programs halt and viewers are reminded of their religious duty.

The government broadcasting station built by President Nasser towers above the Nile in the Bulaq district of Cairo. It was designed originally to help unify the new Republic of Egypt created by the Revolution of 1952. More people work in broadcasting in this building than in all the other African and Arab countries put together.

Sports in Egypt

Not surprisingly, in view of the temperature, swimming is popular with young Egyptians, both in the Mediterranean Sea and in the Nile.

One of the most remarkable developments in Egypt recently, as in several other of the Middle Eastern countries, has been the rapid growth in popularity of soccer—now probably the favorite sport of the region. The Egyptians had seen British servicemen playing soccer since Victorian times, but it did not really catch on either as a game to play or to watch until television came to Egypt. Now even toddlers play, and major playing fields have been constructed. The stadium at Nasr City, on the Cairo airport road, has a capacity of 100,000. It is regularly filled for weekly matches during the soccer season.

Gezirah, the island in the Nile in the middle of Cairo, is equipped for sports ranging from horse racing and golf to soccer, tennis, and swimming.

12 Egypt's Gifts to the World

Even if nobody had lived there after the time of the pharaohs, Egypt had already earned by then its position in history as one of the first places in the world where a major and long-lasting civilization developed. The remains of that civilization are so beautiful and strange that when they have been exhibited in New York or London tens of thousands of people who seldom go near museums have stood in line to see them.

A center of learning

The achievements of Egypt did not stop when the Greeks and Romans took over as rulers. Alexandria itself became one of the great centers of learning of the ancient world, and some ideas we consider basic today developed there. For example, Eratosthenes, the head of the Academy there in the third century B.C., not only understood that the planet Earth is round but also measured its size. By measuring the sun's angle at Alexandria and using geometry, he postulated that the distance around the Earth was 250,000 stades. That is roughly 28,500 miles (46,000 kilometers). Since the Earth is actually about 25,000 miles (just over 40,000 kilometers), his result is very good considering that all he had for his measurement was a simple sundial.

Much of the scientific knowledge of the ancient world was forgotten in Europe until about the fifteenth century. However, in Egypt, the Islamic

The ancient Egyptians were surprisingly skilled in medicine, and some of their knowledge was passed down through the Greeks to the Arabs, and through them eventually to Western Europeans. This wall carving shows surgeons' instruments and pharmacists' scales.

scholars preserved this knowledge. They also advanced the development of sciences like medicine and chemistry. Egypt was one of the routes by which both the knowledge preserved from the ancient world and the new knowledge created by the Arabs found its way to Europe. This happened during the Renaissance of learning in the West in the fifteenth and sixteenth centuries.

Egyptian influences in art and architecture

During Renaissance times, Islamic styles also influenced the Europeans, even as far away as England. The kind of flat-headed arch that became popular in Tudor England at the time of Henry VIII (1509-1547) had been used long before in famous mosques, such as that of al Azhar. From the time of Napoleon's invasion through the nineteenth century, the imagination of North Americans and Europeans was caught by ancient Egypt. Tourism started to become popular, and visitors were fascinated by the temples, tombs, and art of ancient Egypt. It became very fashionable to decorate furniture and buildings with "Egyptian" emblems. The idea of Egyptian mummies coming back to life became a favorite theme for horror stories and films. Today Egypt has its own film industry, centered in Cairo, making both documentaries and entertainment films. Although these are seldom seen in the West, Egypt is the major film producer for the Arabic-speaking world. The leading filmmakers include women like Asma al-Bakry, and in recent times women have shown that they can be influential in all the arts in Egypt. Egypt is also the main book publisher for the Arabic-speaking world. There is a lively tradition of novel and poetry writing in Egypt, and again some of the leading authors are women. Some, like Ahdaf Soueif, write in English as well as in Arabic.

Music is popular in Egypt and both Arabic and Western-style classical music is performed at concerts. Classical as well as rock music is recorded in Egypt and helps to spread the fame of Egyptian performers. One Egyptian singer famous throughout the Middle East was Oom Kalthoum, and her recordings still sell well.

Lost folk traditions

These developments in the media of film, television, recording, and publishing have certainly helped to spread the culture of Egypt both among the Egyptians themselves and to other peoples. Sadly, however, they are also destroying some old folk traditions. However, sometimes past and present meet more happily. Although the Great Pyramid is 4,500 years old, the Egyptians use a high-tech computerized light show in their nighttime presentation to tourists. By displaying the skills of ancient and present-day Egypt like this, they illustrate again that Egypt is above all a land of contrasts.

No one knows what the future will bring. However, wages earned overseas in the oil-rich countries have helped to pay for replacing old-style houses made of sun-dried mud bricks with healthier ones built from fired bricks and concrete. It is hoped that in the future Egypt will be able to continue improving the health of its population.

Index

Abu Simbel 23
Alexander the Great 46, 70
Alexandria 8, 46, 70
ancient civilization 5, 34-42, 83
art and architecture 93
Aswan 13, 21
Aswan High Dam 22, 23, 28, 57, 67-68, 81
Atbara 19, 21, 25

Black Land 7, 8, 9, 24-25, 28-33, 61, 73
Blue Nile 20, 21, 25
Bonaparte, Napoleon 15, 48, 52-53
British rule 52, 54-55

Cairo 8, 19, 69-72, 79
cities 19, 69-72
Cleopatra 46
climate 12-14, 20
  rainfall 12-13, 16, 20
coastline 16-17
communications 29, 42, 70-71, 89
Copts 48-50
cotton industry 30, 65
currency 6

de Lesseps, Ferdinand 53, 54
deserts 12, 14-15, 18
disease 23, 72, 79-81
dress 88

Eastern Highlands 12, 16-17, 74
economy 55, 60, 62-63, 87-88
education 77-78, 82
  of women 82
emigration 5, 82, 86
employment 71, 82, 83, 86-88
energy sources 22, 66-68
explorers 42
exports 63, 65

family life 76, 82, 85
farming 15, 20-21, 27, 28-29, 31, 32
Fayyum Oasis 15, 70
fellahin (peasant farmers) 8, 79
film industry 93
flag 6
food 85, 88
food production 27, 29-31
  cash crops 30, 31
foreign rule, 45-48, 52-53, 54-55
France 30, 52-53, 57

gas production 66-67
geology 14-15, 16
government 59-60
greenhouse effect 27

health care 72, 78, 79-81
hieroglyphic writing 40, 41
housing 72, 80-81
hydroelectricity 67-68

industry 55-56, 64-68
Iraq 6

irrigation 32-33, 68
Islam 46-47, 50-51, 84-85, 89
Israel 56-57, 58

Jordan 86

Khamaseen 13-14

Lake Nasser 22, 23, 28, 68
language 5, 6, 44, 50-51
Libya 60
life expectancy 78-79
literature 93
location 6, 42, 70, 71

mining 16, 17-18
Mubarak, Hosni 60
mummies 17
music 93, 94

Nasser, Gamal Abdul 6, 56, 57
new towns 81
Nile delta 26-27, 73
Nile River 6, 7, 8, 9, 19-27, 75
  flooding 20, 21-22
Nubia 22, 23, 71

oases 15, 70
oil 5, 17, 66-67

Palestine 56
pharaohs 5, 35, 43
pollution 27, 72
population 6, 29, 61-62, 76-77
Port Said 73

pyramids 5, 38-40, 94

Qattara Depression 15

Ramadan 85
Red Lands 8, 9, 12-18
rural life 28-29, 73

Sadat, Anwar al 57-59
Saudi Arabia 6, 62
Sinai Peninsula 12, 16, 56-57, 58
Six Day War 57
Soviet Union 22, 56, 57, 60
sports 90
standard of living 62-63
Suez Canal 7, 53-54, 58, 70, 73, 75
Syria 6, 57, 60

television and radio 29, 89
tourism 16, 17, 73, 83-84, 93
trade 29, 30-31, 62, 63, 67
transportation 74-75
Tutankhamen 37, 38, 43

United Kingdom 54, 55-56
United States 30, 50, 56, 57, 58, 60

wars 15, 16, 55-56, 57
water supply 72, 80, 81
Western Desert 14-15, 74
White Nile 20, 21, 25

© Heinemann Children's Reference 1990
This edition orginally published 1990 by
Heinemann Children's Reference, a division
of Heinemann Educational Books, Ltd.